The Anatomy of
South African Misery

THE WHIDDEN LECTURES
1956

The Anatomy of
South African Misery

BY
C. W. DE KIEWIET

LONDON
OXFORD UNIVERSITY PRESS
NEW YORK TORONTO

Oxford University Press, Amen House, London E.C.4
GLASGOW NEW YORK TORONTO MELBOURNE WELLINGTON
BOMBAY CALCUTTA MADRAS KARACHI
CAPE TOWN IBADAN NAIROBI ACCRA SINGAPORE

FIRST EDITION 1956
REPRINTED 1957 (TWICE)

PRINTED IN GREAT BRITAIN

Contents

Foreword

THE WHIDDEN LECTURES honour the memory of the late Reverend Howard P. Whidden, D.D., LL.D., D.C.L., F.R.S.C., 1871–1952, Chancellor[1] of McMaster University from 1923 to 1941.

A member of a family resident in Antigonish since 1761, after earlier settlement in New England in 1700, Dr. Whidden was born in Nova Scotia. He graduated in Arts from Acadia University (1891) and in Theology from McMaster (1894), subsequently studying at the University of Chicago. He was the minister of Baptist churches in Ontario, Manitoba, and Ohio, and from 1913 to 1923 President of Brandon College in Manitoba, that college being at that time affiliated with McMaster University. He had previously been a member of its teaching staff from 1900 to 1903. He served in the House of Commons in Ottawa from 1917 to 1921 as the Union Government member for Brandon.

Under his leadership, McMaster University was removed in 1930 from Toronto to Hamilton. The immediate onset of the depression, followed by World War II, created added anxiety, but, throughout, he retained his graciousness and courage, and the foundation he laid has proved to be a sound one. He is remembered as a man of striking appearance, unusual dignity, ready tolerance, deep conviction and broad educational outlook.

The lectures were endowed in 1954 through the gift of E. C. Fox, B.A., LL.D., of Toronto, who was a mem-

[1] The title of this office was changed in 1950 to President and Vice-Chancellor.

ber of the Board of Governers during Dr. Whidden's tenure of office, and Chairman of the Building and Executive Committees. The fund is to be used within the discretion of the Board, except that for ten years it is to be employed to bring to the University scholars of note, who will endeavour to bridge the gap between the older Arts disciplines and the various fields of scientific inquiry.

The first lectures on the foundation were delivered in January, 1956, by Cornelis Willem de Kiewiet, M.A., PH.D., LL.D., L.H.D., President of the University of Rochester, New York. His choice of subject, *The Anatomy of South African Misery*, was dictated not only by the current interest in the problem of colour in the Union of South Africa, but by his own long connexion with that country. Born in Holland, he spent his youth in South Africa, graduating from the University of Witwatersrand in 1923. He holds the Ph.D. degree from the University of London, where he studied as Herbert Ainsworth Scholar in Modern History, with later studies at the Universities of Paris and Berlin. He taught in Southern Rhodesia from 1923 to 1925, thereafter going to the state university of Iowa from 1929 to 1941, and to Cornell University from 1941 to 1951. Successively Professor of Modern European History, Dean of the College of Arts and Science, Provost and Acting President at Cornell, he became President of the University of Rochester in 1951.

Dr. de Kiewiet's writings include *The Imperial Factor* (Cambridge 1937), *A History of South Africa* (Oxford

1941), and three chapters in the *Cambridge History of the British Empire* (Cambridge 1937). In the field of American History, he has written with reference to the constitution and foreign policy. During World War II he served as Director of Army Specialized Training Program at Cornell University and special consultant to the Navy Department. In 1947 he conducted for the Carnegie Corporation a study of South African educational institutions, and in 1951 was Director of Study on Economic, Political and Social Conditions in East Africa, for the Carnegie Corporation and the Institute of International Education. From 1950 to 1952 he was a member of the Advisory Committee on Underdeveloped Areas, Mutual Security Agency, and from 1951 to 1954 a member of the Commission on Human Resources and Advanced Training, for the Rockefeller Foundation and National Research Council. He is now a member of the African Study Fellowship Screening Committee of the Ford Foundation, and a member of the New York State Committee for White House Conference on Education. Among other honours, he is an Officer of the Legion of Honour.

Dr. de Kiewiet's plea for a more humane and farsighted approach to the problem of Africa sheds light on the larger problem of human relations that appears with greater or less intensity throughout the world to-day.

G. P. GILMOUR

THE PRESIDENT'S OFFICE,
MCMASTER UNIVERSITY,
HAMILTON, CANADA.
May, 1956.

I

Nationalism and Racialism

I AM PROUD to be the scholar to inaugurate this distinguished Whidden Lecture series. I claim the privilege of commending the wisdom and the statesmanship of Dr. Edward Carey Fox's gift to McMaster University, and of giving all the prominence that lies in my power to the hope that as Canada advances in prosperity, as inevitably she will, those who own or control her wealth, will cause a generous share to flow to the support of the Canadian universities. The idea of the University, the idea of truth, and the idea of human liberty have common origins and to-day cannot be disengaged. To harm or constrain any one, is to harm or constrain all. In a sense these three lectures are based upon a belief in the truth of these statements.

It is my hope that this audience will understand and accept the mention in these lectures of the name of another man. A few weeks ago I was standing in the lobby of a London hotel when with a start of glad surprise I caught sight of a man whom I consider the outstanding personality in South African university life. In an environment where these things are no longer easy he was more than anybody else the spokesman for the great ideas of the University, truth and human liberty. Principal Davie of the University of Cape Town was the profile of courage itself. As he stood beside me he carried within his own physical body nature's warning that he had drawn far too heavily upon his energy and his courage. As a physician he knew that the wounds which he carried within himself were deep and dangerous. Men are forgiven if they become jealous of the treasure of life and guard it against any further dissipation or curtailment. In the hours that followed our meeting, we who were his friends tried in vain to steer him away from what I have here called the anatomy of South African misery. But his conviction, his eloquence and his anger were a harness he had placed upon himself. Simply he said, "As long as I can get to my feet I shall fight." When he learned that I had the manuscript of these lectures with me he demanded to see it, and painfully hobbled after me to get it. I left the lectures with him, pleased at his interest, but nervous, for I had no other copy.

When I returned to the United States the manuscript lay on my desk. On the first few pages he had made suggestions for its improvement. But the shaking hand did not write very far. Tom Davie died with these lectures beside him. A country or a cause is poor that has no men like Tom Davie. I like to feel that a note of his voice will be in mine, and that his approval rests upon my words.

I am doubly proud to appear before you as an historian, speaking on the greatest of all themes—the relations between human beings. But I am also fearful. The study of history is a training in humility. After more than twenty-five years of study and writing I am impressed by the great difficulty of being an historian.

Of all disciplines it is the most exacting and laborious. Few disciplines require a longer apprenticeship. The function of history is to put wisdom and experience at the disposal of each generation. A vigorous and independent historiography is more than an ornament of culture. It is the indispensable agent to wise and successful action in all human problems. In the world of scholarship the historian's craft comes the closest to statesmanship. Without historians a society cannot be mature or make its decisions wisely. Between democracy and a free inspired historiography there is a real equation. Amongst disciplines it is the greatest emancipator, releasing men from thraldom to the past, setting free their minds and their hearts for the tasks of each new generation. The historian at his desk sheds hypocrisy in human relations, and is the declared enemy of what Norman Angell once called the unseen assassins— the words that defeat truth and accurate understanding by their prejudice or their falsity. In its fullness history is the meeting place of all knowledge.

At this time and especially in this University, I want to issue a plea on behalf of what used to be called imperial studies, and what to-day are more properly called Commonwealth studies. Great changes have befallen the British Empire so that some even speak of its decline and fall. Precisely because the British Empire is giving way to new societies and the travail of their emergence is great and dangerous, it is all the more necessary to cultivate the study of these great transformations.

3

My admiration for the great British Universities is high, yet it has always been qualified because not till after the Second World War was a proper effort made to realize the late Victorian promise of an era of vigorous and creative imperial studies. In not one of the British Universities did scholarship in the greatest expansion of cultural influence since the Roman Empire acquire the dignity and the stature of the great traditional fields like medieval or constitutional history. When I first arrived in London thirty years ago, eager at the prospect of studying in its great archives and libraries, I was struck by the secondariness of imperial studies, a status which was never discussed and about which nobody quarreled. The incumbent of the most distinguished chair in Imperial Studies in all of Great Britain baffled his students by doing most of his research in Tudor constitutional history, and I was not the only student from the Dominions to feel that unless I had listened to Tawney on economic history or Pollard on constitutional history I had not experienced British historical scholarship at its best. Taken by themselves these are trivial reminiscences, and could even seem ungracious comments on a rich and rewarding experience in my own intellectual life. They are meaningful because the failure to invest the study of the British Empire and Commonwealth with the stature, the intellectual excitement, the diversity and the imaginativeness which it deserved, is related to the inattentiveness, the misunderstanding and the error with which the affairs of the Empire and the Commonwealth have sometimes

4

been conducted. In no field is this statement more meaningful than in Africa.

The modern world has formed an attentive ring about the affairs of Africa. The problems of Africa from Casablanca to Cape Town have become world problems that are freely debated in Peking and Delhi, Moscow and Washington. In the shift of power that is taking place in the modern world Africa's raw materials, lines of communication, military staging areas and bases, have been raised to a new level of significance. All of Africa has acquired the strategic importance that once belonged especially to the Straits of Gibraltar, the Suez Canal and the Cape of Good Hope. In Asia the colonial Empires of the Netherlands, France and Great Britain are reaching the final stages of a revolutionary transfer of power to former colonial peoples. Every step in the vast reassessment of the traditional relationships between peoples and races is being watched by a strained and anxious generation, hungry for relief from danger and sacrifice, yet aware also that the shifts of power and the emergence of new societies incessantly carry the danger of war. The world is undertaking a new approach to man. It has embarked on a search for more freedom for more people. Because there is disagreement on the nature of freedom and the manner in which it may be attained the steps taken towards emancipation may also stumble into disaster. It is revealing to contrast the polite inattentiveness of the atmosphere in which the British North America Act was passed almost ninety years ago with the acutely controversial atmosphere in which all modern political and constitutional debate must take place. Until the second World War the colonial powers were under no severe compulsion through domestic or world opinion to undertake major political, economic or social reform.

To-day the course of history has brought all Africa to the end of the period of quietude. Events within and without Africa have made its political and racial problems into major factors in world politics. Initiative has passed into the hands of new powers like India who insist on being the energetic spokesmen for the remaining coloured and subject races of the world. The historic meeting at Bandoeng of representatives of Asian and African peoples was eloquent testimony of the new self-awareness and the assertiveness of non-Western peoples. The spectacular tour through India, Burma and Afghanistan of the heads of the Russian state must be seen for what it really is: the recognition by astute and designing men that the unrest and the ineluctable flow of events in Asia and Africa constitute the greatest phenomenon of our time.

A substantial measure of initiative has also passed into the hands of the African native population. The Gold Coast is engaged upon a critical experiment in self-rule. Nigeria is passing through the quarrels and dissensions which traditionally accompany the constitution-making of the British Commonwealth. In Central Africa three territories have come together in a political federation and a social experiment in inter-racial co-operation. On the surface and beneath it a long list of unrelated events reveals an unrest from which no part of the continent is free. The sum of all the items of protest, great and small, is impressive. Africa south of the Sahara is not Asia, and is not yet on the verge of revolution. Discontent does not yet speak with discontent across the many frontiers in a common language of protest. Yet the tide of events in Africa runs ever more swiftly. Already Africa is a principal area of racial conflict. The manner in which the west handles Africa will widen or lessen the opportunities of the communist powers, and influence the degree of Asia's reconciliation with the west.

This is the background against which the race problems of the Union of South Africa must be seen. The efforts in South Africa to maintain and reinforce the ascendancy of its white population over the non-white population of Africans, Indians, and coloured men is in conflict with what is nothing less than a major revolution in racial relations in the modern world. The world is still full of the discriminations of race, colour and creed. But it is no longer indifferent or complacent. We are beginning to recognize more fully that when men are compelled to live within a rigid class, confined within an exclusive creed, or subjected to discrimination of race and colour, they are less worthy as men and less valuable as citizens. Imposed discrimination restricts access to the law and education, to health and entertainment, to dignity and progress. It starves hope and feeds anger. Therefore, in spite of law and convention the racial policies of South Africa have lost their domestic character and have become a leading issue in

7

international relations. The word *apartheid* has entered into the official propaganda of communist nations, and into the daily vocabulary of millions of people. History supports the view that no society can insulate itself against the life and experience of its neighbours. Every inhabitant of the Gold Coast who casts a free ballot, every native of the Congo who drives a locomotive, every native of Uganda, or Tanganyika who independently raises and sells cotton or coffee in the world market, every native worker in a northern Rhodesia copper mine who strikes against his company, becomes unconsciously and remotely a critic of South Africa's racial policies, establishing contradictions and alternatives which all the world may observe and which no frontier patrol can prevent from entering into the minds of South Africa's own native population.

Because Africa is swiftly moving from obscurity into crisis the study of its history has become an urgent necessity. To-day men are much in need of a key to the difficult and dangerous racial policies of the Union of South Africa.

An understanding of the Boer War is the gateway to most of the issues of modern South Africa. More than any other single event the Boer War intensified, complicated and embittered the already ensnarled relationships of Boer and Briton, Bantu and Indian, white and non-white. In South African history the Boer War combines some of the qualities of the American Revolutionary War and some of the qualities of the Civil War. It ended the regime of separate colonies and republics and led to the establishment of the Union. But it was also virtually a civil war between the Dutch and the English. In America after the Civil War truculence and resentment deprived the defeated southern states of the ability and willingness to keep pace with the new thought and action which were building American industrial democracy. The accursed legacy of the Civil War was the anachronistic thought and the historical lag which result when men are preoccupied with defeat and ancient grievance. It is the bitter paradox of modern South African history that the war which united the country politically divided it racially.

Like all wars the Boer War was a tragedy, born of error and human failing. It was the bloody price which both British and Dutch had to pay in order to mend the errors of almost a century, and in order to cement the unity without which neither peace nor prosperity were possible. The failure of both the Boer republican and British governments to prevent the economic and social problems of gold mining from becoming political and diplomatic issues was the basic cause of war. If the old Cape Colony had been at all industrialized it could have served as a training ground in the ways of the industrial revolution and investment capital. But the Cape Colony had no experienced engineers or bankers or business men who could step into the troubled atmosphere of the Witwatersrand and swiftly begin the work of mediation which alone could prevent tragedy. Instead the inexperienced South African Republic had to avail itself of the services of non-South African Hollanders like Dr. Leyds whose lack of sympathy with the motley throng on the gold fields led him to apply the procedures and stratagems of competitive international diplomacy to the issues of South Africa.

In our generation it has become difficult to recall the atmosphere of the closing Victorian generation, or to imagine the massive and apparently indestructible shape of Great Britain which gave the Englishman an unshakeable feeling of superiority and rectitude. Of the agents of the new industrial age ushered in by gold and diamonds some were vulgar and arrogant men, with the illusion that their worth as persons was equal to the great forces which they commanded. Some of those who came to South Africa and the gold fields failed to recognize or respect the inner life of the men who had founded the Boer Republics. They gave offence, often deep and cruel, to men whose pride and dignity, or ideas of happiness and success could not be measured by the standards of Birmingham or Threadneedle Street.

To men like Cecil Rhodes and Jameson, Great Britain was a phenomenon so universal and commanding that it became the climate in which they breathed, a habit of their own mind, investing them with the task of completing a great imaginative work, the advancement of the Empire. The fault was not in their vision but in the tools they used. Seen at the distance of more than half a century, and through the unhappy blur of war, Rhodes' vision of expansion and integration seems even more logical to-day that it did then. Once the industrial revolution had arrived with its railroads, investments and world markets southern Africa required wholeness and integration, not separateness and conflict. But Rhodes was too impetuous and ruthless, and his followers too contemptuous of their opponents, to know that the new wholeness had first of all to be created in the minds of men. This could be done only through negotiation and consent. [The fault of men like Paul Kruger was that they did not see that Rhodes was on the side of the future. The fault of Rhodes and his followers was that they did not see how much Kruger was governed by the past.] Contempt, treachery and violence were acids that deeply and indelibly etched the record of the differences that had divided English and Dutch since the beginning of the century. By ignoring the logic of the future and the lessons of the past between them they brought on the Boer War.

The Jameson Raid of 1895 is a classic illustration of the insensitive and arrogant attitude of those who opposed Paul Kruger. The Jameson Raid was a freebooting attempt to end the involved problem of the gold fields by overturning the government of Paul Kruger, and thus creating a situation in which British intervention and control over the South African Republic would have been inevitable. The plot failed ignominiously. The story of bungling and clumsy conspiracy is a familiar one. Because the Jameson Raid was a failure it was also an affront. Nothing could have done more to turn the obstinacy of Paul Kruger's regime into a bitter intractability, or to deepen an already acute feeling of wrong.

The Republican leaders in the Transvaal were convinced that the Colonial Secretary, Joseph Chamberlain, and the British Government were active parties to the plot. Historians are still trying to bring order and clarity into the fog of evasion, denials, disappearing documents and the manipulations by tight-lipped men which obscured the truth. One of my most dramatic moments as an historian came when I first saw the almost blank sheet of paper which is part of the evidence of the complicity of Joseph Chamberlain and the Colonial Office in this unworthy effort of the government of a great Empire to solve its problems by rapine, and then to hide its complicity by helping to engineer a lie which no later generosity or statesmanship could wholly purge. The brutality of the Jameson Raid and the cynical dishonesty which followed it became a barrier which the angrier and less forgiving spirits amongst the Dutch refused to cross. The historian best knows that a lack of explanation of any notorious circumstance can become a wound that will not heal, or an offending emptiness across which men cannot reach one another. Such a wound and such an emptiness existed for two generations in the true history of the causes of the Boer War. Unconfessed guilt is an enemy of tranquility in men and societies. Better that Joseph Chamberlain had lost office, or that the whole British Cabinet had fallen than to brazen through so sorry a deceit. Under the British parliamentary system it is the fall of governments as well as their formation which provides valuable education and enlightenment in political affairs. A Colonial Secretary or even a Cabinet would have been a small price to pay in order to avoid the resentment and disaster that followed. The failure of the Jameson Raid to precipitate a major Cabinet crisis was a measure of the secondariness of colonial issues. It demonstrated the illiteracy of Parliament in the affairs of the Empire, and the absence of men in British political life who would stand toe-to-toe with Joseph Chamberlain in one of those debates that on other issues were the strength and the glory of British nineteenth century parliamentary govenment. Had the Cabinet fallen there might have been no Boer War.

The Boer War was a little war. Yet it was a critical event in contemporary history. It became a significant chapter in the textbook of anti-capitalist and anti-imperialist criticism. Marxist and Leninist analysis seized upon it with enthusiasm as a classic vindication of their contentions. In the vital generation before the first World War it spurred the forces of neutralism in countries like the Netherlands and of isolationism in the United States. It revealed that the great strength and prestige of Great Britain did not depend upon the ability to wage and win wars, but upon the ability to maintain the peace. For Great Britain, of all powers, any war, no matter what its military outcome, was the prelude to loss of prestige and to national decline. The outbreak of war in 1899 or 1914 or 1939 was in each case a form of defeat that no military victory could correct.

The greatest error and sinning of the responsible men

in Great Britain who accepted the possibility of war in South Africa instead of forbidding it, was in their betrayal of the deepest and most genuine of all British interests—the Pax Britannica itself. Not through her great navy, her worldwide trade or exports of investment capital, not through her industrial might and world-wide possessions, was Great Britain the leading figure in the contemporary world. Her continued primacy depended in the very first place upon her ability to keep faith with the deeply true and moral persuasion of Richard Cobden and John Bright and the many who followed them, that the first ally of the British Empire was peace, even as its greatest enemy was war. How profoundly true this statement is, our generation well knows, for the modern world is applying the same anxious test to the leadership of the United States. America's vast wealth, her industrial might, her stockpile of hydrogen bombs, her strategic bases and industrious foreign policy are not admired as a preparation for war or as the means of winning a war, but only as the means of maintaining the peace. The Boer War speeded the growing forces of unfriendliness around Great Britain, dampened the belief in the peaceable quality of British life and policy, weakened the adherence of men's minds to her causes. Worst of all it marked a definite stage in the rising tide of criticism of colonial relations within and without Great Britain that encouraged a sense of guilt in some and of doubt in others. A sense of guilt and doubt drained Great Britain's imperial policies of their Victorian conviction and resoluteness. In my own generation as a student in Great Britain it was clear that the secondary status of imperial studies was associated in decisive intellectual and political circles in Great Britain with feelings of dissent, and even repudiation. How greatly these feelings caused a relaxation of the national will, and how greatly they limited the accumulation of the scholarly knowledge and experience vitally necessary to meet the coming crisis in Africa we shall never fully know.

[Each succeeding generation in South Africa has learned more of the unfortunate legacy of resentment and rancour left by the Boer War.] The British have learned more fully than any other people that the method by which power is transferred is at least as important as the transfer of power itself. It is a commonplace that Great Britain learned a lesson in the American Revolution that she wisely applied to Canada, New Zealand, Australia, and now in our own generation to India, Pakistan, Burma and the Gold Coast. Power gained through violence and revolt is marked by passions that endure for generations. It is instructive to place side by side the historiography of the British North America Act with that of the War of American Independence, or to contrast the establishment of Irish self-rule with that of India. Indian historians will not write the history of their country around a war of emancipation or a bloody revolution as a focus of patriotism and nationalist passion. This may become one of the most influential factors in modern history. [In South Africa it is not the peaceful Act of Union of

1909, but the Boer War which nationalist historians consider the foundation experience of the nation. The British post-war settlement after 1902 was distinguished by generosity and the final wisdom of the Act of Union. Yet the occurrence of the Boer War made difficult the full recognition of the fact that the post-war settlement and the Act of Union were a peaceful and voluntary transfer of power comparable with the British North America Act. The pain of war left a hunger for a compensating victory, for a retroactive declaration of independence, for some symbolic act of rebellion and defiance that would purge the memory of defeat and wrong. A war and not a peaceful constitution became the seedbed of nationalist feeling and racial passion.

After the Boer War the best minds in Great Britain had some of the wisdom of the East Roman Empire in admitting the nobility of subjugated peoples to equality with the Byzantine nobility. To this day the Prime Minister of the Union of South Africa has never been an Englishman. This is important evidence of the essential honesty and broadmindedness of the post-war political settlement. On the Dutch side Botha, Hofmeyr and later Smuts recognised that the nineteenth century was ended, and that there was no problem that was not best handled in a spirit of reconciliation and co-operation. In 1914 they carried the logic of reconciliation to the point of becoming the fighting allies of Great Britain.

In the post-war settlement there was one flaw or deficiency which was increasingly regarded as a fresh affront to the dignity of the Afrikaner people. The secondariness of the Afrikaans language and culture was perhaps an understandable consequence of military defeat. It was, however, interpreted as evidence that the money and effort of reconstruction were put to the service of racial and cultural domination instead of genuine racial co-operation. This belief explains why a section of the Afrikaner population looked upon the conduct of men like Smuts as faithless and even traitorous. In the generation before the first World War the primacy of the English language and culture seemed to have the self-evident qualities of natural law. Because the history of the British Empire did not rank with constitutional or classical history in the education of Englishmen the story of French Canada after the Durham Report seemed to have little influence on Milner and his hard-working colleagues.

The criticism of the cultural policies of the reconstruction regime can be driven too far. Poetry and law, history and science, individual genius and the grandeur of traditional ceremonial, the triumphs of war and the great crises in the growth of constitutional freedom and the liberal conscience gave powers to the British tongue and culture which the men and laws of a short generation could not reduce. Nor should a later enthusiasm for Afrikaans language and culture hide the truth that after the Boer War their status was in fact secondary and ambiguous. At that time the language of education, of the pulpit and ceremony was the language of the Netherlands. Uncertainty and confusion in the minds

17

of the Afrikaner population must accept some measure of the blame for the lesser status of their language and culture.

The great merit of Smuts and his followers was their emancipation from the isolationism of the Boer Republics, and their recognition that no country can stand aside from the great tide of the world's history. They were willing to trade a century of wrong for a new century of hope. The acceptance by Botha and Smuts after the Boer War of the task of building a more homogeneous and compatible European community contained an implicit willingness to leave the way open to those new influences of which the English language and culture were the principal vehicle. In spite of his great insights Smuts made no creative contribution to the native question. Yet a reconciled and united European community was the indispensable preliminary to confronting the other great social and racial questions of the Union. Failure would mean flight from the twentieth century, a withdrawal into cultural isolation, the establishment of a divisive nationalism, refusal to accept the new social and political philosophy that elsewhere in the modern world was leading to emancipation, to a mitigation of racial conflict, and to the elevation of the political and economic status of subject peoples.

The success of Smuts and his followers was considerable, yet amongst the population which they tried to lead away from the Boer War into the new future there were from the very beginning men who made concessions reluctantly or not at all. The slow and persistent rise of an aggressive Afrikaner nationalism after the Boer War has many sources and diverse explanations. The architects of the new nationalism were scholars and Boer War generals, ministers of the gospel and farmers, landless men and journalists. An honourable determination to reaffirm the pride of language, race and history combined with a fiercer resolve to avenge failure and humiliation. Afrikaners with the strongest sense of grievance developed a special feeling of innocence and rectitude, which blocked their ability to envisage a society, hospitable to all men, or to discern error in themselves. Evil and error were outside themselves, in British imperialism, in the gold mining corporations, in the new industrial towns, in the backward native population. To a hard and irreconcilable core the decision of Botha and Smuts to enter the first World War on the British side was an act of betrayal. As the economic costs of war were felt in rising prices and shortages, the policies of Botha and Smuts were vilified as a turncoat surrender to the same imperialism and capitalist greed which had caused the Boer War. The first World War widened a rift that could never again be closed. The post-war depression and the decline of British power encouraged the rapid growth of the new Afrikaner nationalism.

The waning prestige of Great Britain and the mounting disorder in Europe which finally precipitated the second World War created an atmosphere propitious to the forces in Asia, the Middle East and elsewhere that sought to adjust their relations with the British

Empire. By the outbreak of the second World War the extreme wing of the Afrikaner nationalist movement had become frankly a movement to capture control in politics and predominance in culture. The more militant advocates of Afrikaner nationalism were willing to accept the possibility of British defeat in the second World War as a means of establishing political independence and racial ascendancy. It was before and during the second World War that imitation of Nazi vocabulary and political behaviour suddenly revealed the authoritarian and ruthless will to power that had developed in the extreme form of Afrikaner nationalism.

It was a part of the humiliation of defeat in the Boer War that it had been inflicted in the presence of an inferior and subject race, of whom the Boers felt they were the masters both by conquest and cultural superiority. Racism in the American South was greatly worsened by the Civil War. The Civil War and the great political conflicts that followed turned the negro into a scapegoat, and made his true emancipation through education and citizenship the arduous and unfinished problem of the next hundred years.

The relations between Afrikaner and British in South Africa cannot be fully compared with the relations between Fleming and Walloon in Belgium or French and English in Canada. In the background of war and constitution making was always the great non-white population of natives, Indians and mixed breeds or coloured men. And it was against these that Afrikaner nationalism drew its sharpest frontiers. Afrikaner nationalism is an instrument of cultural defence against the English and of racial defence against the natives. Although racial discrimination in South Africa is emphatically not confined to the Afrikaner population alone, yet it has special roots in the history and experience of the Afrikaner population.

In the eighteenth century, slavery in the old Cape Colony developed the same familism which was so effective in Brazil and the Southern United States in assimilating the negro to Brazilian or American civilization. The American negro slave in 1860 on the eve of the Civil War was closer to being an American than he was to being an African. Almost as certainly the original Cape slave population by the time of its final emancipation in 1838 were less Hottentot or Malay than members of the colonial community. But the Great Trek brought the emigrant Boers into contact with the organized tribes of the interior. With these they entered upon a generation of conflict and bloodshed, so that every South African schoolboy is taught to place an altogether exaggerated emphasis upon war and conflict because of the long lists of native wars which he has to learn.

The men who trekked into the interior had two objectives: the first was free and peaceful use of land and water for their cattle and sheep. This objective led them to establish their ascendancy over the pastoral tribes by force of arms. But the second major purpose of the migration into the interior was to establish a society in which "proper relations" between master and servant could be maintained. Cheap land and cheap labour were the twin fruits of victory over the tribes. The outcome of a generation of wars and skirmishes was to bring the native population within the economy of the white man. The proper comparison of the settlement of South Africa is not with the Indian wars of America or Canada, but with those phases of Arab or Spanish expansion which led to the subjugation of other races for purposes of tribute and cheap tractable labour, and to the establishment of new societies in which economic and social superiority is sustained by a division of society into two economic and political classes. The incorporation of the native population as a cheap labour force, but segregated by political rightlessness and severe social discrimination, is the single most important key to an understanding of all subsequent social and economic developments. The two Boer republics were democratic in their political discussion and in their lawmaking. But they contained no patrician element or privileged economic group which might have made the cause of the native populations its special interest. The creation of a society composed of a master class and a servant class was further reinforced by the version of Calvinism which withholds the full grace of God from the native. In our own generation the persuasion that the inferiority of the African native is incurable is considered intellectually obsolete, politically unwise, economically unprofitable, and morally reprehensible. In human affairs most forms of discrimination are pessimistic in character. Many of the influences that have worked in the formation of Afrikaner nationalism and culture have been pessimistic and defensive rather than optimistic. The strain of Calvinism in Afrikaner political and social thought is clearly pessimistic. It is pessimism that co-operates with the feelings of innocence and rectitude that mark Afrikaner nationalism. The belief that native inferiority is inborn leads to the conclusion that the evils of native existence are not the result of human errors that could be mitigated or corrected. Ignorance and disease are marks of an inner defect in the native, and the struggle against poverty, ignorance and disease is the responsibility of those who suffer from them. Their own keen doctrine of freedom was strictly for themselves and they had no responsibility to include the natives in its realm. Man could not grant a hope which God himself had denied. Since all men were not equal before God they could not be equal in the presence of one another. It therefore became difficult to recognize the man-made character of slums and demoralization, most difficult especially to acquire the optimism which is the driving force of all reform.

One of the most telling facts in South African history is the absence in the nineteenth century Afrikaner population of a reform movement in the field of race relations, where ringing and rebellious voices were raised against popular belief and practice. The withdrawal from the old Cape Colony meant that there was no party in the republic with roots in humanitarianism or the philosophic optimism of the eighteenth century to soften the asperity of Voortrekker Calvinism. Because the republics had few schools and no higher education they never received the optimistic intellectual impact of the science and technology of the nineteenth century. It was the scientific and industrial development of the nineteenth century that gave the optimism of the eighteenth century a new vigour and fresh justification, and gave men the conviction that they could master their environment and improve the social conditions in which they lived. To men like Paul Kruger science and technology were alien forces, harsh and greedy in their conduct to the point of assaulting the freedom of the republic and plunging it into war. The war that ended the nineteenth century reinforced the spirit of withdrawal and pessimism which the nineteenth century had produced. But Afrikaner nationalism now also claimed to be the instrument of racial survival, the ark of God's covenant with the Afrikaner people, the protective armour of white civilization in a continent of 150,000,000 blacks, the unyielding foe of cultural degredation or racial mixture. "The Afrikaner nation," said one of its militant leaders, "was placed in this country by God's hand and is destined to remain as a nation with its own character and its own mission."

The new nationalists sought to set themselves off against all others, against black men, Indian and coloured, but also against their English countrymen, as invested with a special corporateness, and an overriding historical mandate. In their vision of the world the maintenance of cultural identity and the preservation of racial purity are the first obligation of the Afrikaner people and the government they establish.

24

Wisdom and righteousness come from those who know and accept God's will in establishing the Christian state of the Afrikaner people as the ordained instrument for protecting their nationalism and their racial purity. In the language of South African Calvinism God is sovereign and has delegated sovereignty to the lawful rulers of the land. For these rulers right action is self-evident and does not come from free political debate or a scrutiny of the wisdom and experience of other societies. It does not call for a regime of broadening political opportunities for all who are ruled, least of all if they are Indians, coloured men and natives whose race is a menace to the purity which the state is pledged to defend. In such a context it is important to recognize that all questions, whatever their real nature, are first of all political, cultural and racial. A special theory is developed in which the economic life of society is subordinated to its political objectives, so that non-European workers are not free to improve their standard of living if thereby they seek also to gain added political opportunity or social advancement. The economy of South Africa is ruled by political and racial considerations to an extent that is unusual in most western democracies. The place and share which individuals and groups enjoy in the economy are not the result of the services which they render but of their racial and political status.

The initiative of Afrikaner nationalism was encouraged by the failure after 1918 to maintain a flow of bright and thrusting young minds from Great Britain. The slaughter of some of the flower of British youth punished more parts of the Empire than South Africa, for they never received again as generous a share of Great Britain's aspiring and creative minds. In fact, there was a debilitating seepage of talent back to Great Britain. The period between the wars saw the active growth of separate Afrikaans-speaking universities. The Afrikaans universities are perhaps more truly South African than the English-speaking universities, which have not always dared escape from a sort of minor British provincialism. Universities in a new land are especially in need of daring and enterprise. In the vital field of race relations, there was in the English-speaking universities insufficient enterprise or daring. In the critical period between the two world wars they lost the chance of becoming a common and generous meeting ground where the equal intercourse of eager youth could end the estrangements of the past and seek to dissolve the prejudices of race and colour. Far too heavy a load was placed upon the shoulders of the few men of courage and insight in economics, sociology, and history who laboured to promote the new thought and enterprise out of which South African society could generate the policies and adjustments which were necessary if Afrikaner, English, African, Indian and coloured men were to live harmoniously together.

To a disturbing extent important and aggressive groups within the Afrikaans-speaking universities chose to think and work within the narrow and confining framework of the racial and social policies of an exclusive Afrikaner nationalism. The degeneration of scholarship into partisanship is a familiar phenomenon. It appears in many universities in many lands. But no university can serve its true purpose if the forces within it generate and exact a uniformity of thought and expression in essential things. This is the danger of any university which is devoted to one race, or one faith or one economic or social pattern. It would be a gross distortion not to recognize the warmth and excitement of the intellectual communities at Stellenbosch and Pretoria which were expressing and enhancing the worth of their own language and culture. Nor would it be proper to suggest that the Afrikaans-speaking universities became altogether inhospitable to men of liberal and generous views. Yet the exclusive character of the Afrikaans-speaking universities favoured the policy of winning the greatest measure of authority and pre-eminence for the Afrikaans language and culture, and co-operated with the programme of special political ascendancy for the Afrikaner section of the community. The insistence on separatism within separatism, on emphatic racial and cultural distinctions, gave rise inevitably to the conviction that South African problems were so special that they could neither be compared with nor influenced by the experience of other societies.

No impartial observer of the rise of the more militant forms of Afrikaner racial nationalism can fail to be impressed by a sort of deafness or inattentiveness to history, by the refutation of illuminating analogies, and especially by an unwillingness to seek help and guidance in the rich storehouse of racial experience of other societies. Thus the contemporary voices of experience from Brazil and the United States and the ancient voices from Byzantium or Arab imperialism went unheard. To minds like Prime Minister Strydom or Mr. Verwoerd the suggestion, for example, that the frantic quality of their nationalism has a modern counterpart in Israel would be incomprehensible. Yet Israel, too, to Israelis is a refuge from suffering and a fortress against surrounding enemies.

Historical deafness and an anachronistic preoccupation with the special episodes in their own past confined the more dedicated Afrikaner nationalists to a narrow world of thought and action. They felt they were equally threatened by the rich cultural heritage of the British and the degrading culture of the natives. Their nationalist movement was like a war on two fronts, against domination from above and invasion from below. Security was possible only by a maximum insistence on the separateness of races, language and culture. A new generation began to appear, competent, industrious, resourceful and courageous. Its members were more defiant, and had less of the personal courtesy and sparkling wittiness which had long been a special ornament of the Afrikaans people and language. Even their language which once tripped easily on the tongue became more turgid and massive under the weight of Dutch and Germanic neologisms. There is discernible a tendency, especially in the spheres dominated by a militant Afrikaner nationalism, for knowledge and thought, art and expression to be organized in the special service of white domination. An Afrikaner child can easily graduate from high school without becoming objectively acquainted with the economic and political criticism of the doctrines of *apartheid*. The pursuit and dissemination of knowledge, even certain forms of art insidiously serve the fixed system of racial relations. It is instructive for example to compare the famous Voortrekker monument outside Pretoria with its frank portrayal of nineteenth century relations of master and servant with the rebellious attack on peonage and human subservience in the art of Rivera or Orozco. They also greatly lessened their chances of stepping, as did Jan Smuts, on to the platforms of the Commonwealth and the world as spokesmen for men and nations outside their own shores. The world is poorer because of these things. Their impoverished spirits and limited horizons made it impossible for them to share in the exciting re-education and reassessment which is taking place in the modern world.

For fifty years a screen of gold and diamonds was drawn between men's eyes and the tragedy that was arising before them. South Africa's wealth in diamonds, gold and in recent times uranium obscured the severity and danger of political conflict and racial unwisdom. Minerals gave South Africa an economic progress which made her outstanding amongst all the other territories of Africa south of the Sahara. The net national income was multiplied by more than six times between the time of Union in 1910 and 1949. All the other British territories in Africa combined do not equal the export income of South Africa. Almost half of the foreign capital invested south of the Sahara in Africa has been invested in the Union. Good prices and high employment during long periods maintained a buoyant atmosphere which tempered and muffled the growing racial crisis. Nature's bounty helped make South Africa blind and deaf. During more than two generations the steady and profitable roar of gold mining machinery deafened men to the grief that rose from the hovels at the foot of the great white piles of crushed rock. South Africa never endured the acute and protracted economic depression which led to the revolutionary legislation of the New Deal in the United States or to the spectacular rise of the Labour Party in Great Britain. She was, it is true, briefly and severely touched by the world-wide depression of the 1930's. In consequence she did come to grips with the pathetic problems of poverty and demoralization amongst the poor whites. But depression did not last long enough for men to be forced to see that in the deepest sense the poor blacks were like the poor whites, except that they were more numerous, more voiceless, and more rightless. Bitter and disappointed men have argued that only a devastating depression could bring white South Africa to its senses, by exposing the anatomy of African misery, and frightening it into pity and wisdom.

There is cause for grave concern that South Africa has thus far been unable to develop any significant party, aggressively committed to a liberal solution of

the racial problems. There is no difficulty in developing
the arguments that prove the folly of building a modern
state upon the illiteracy, the inefficiency and the unhappiness of four-fifths of the population. Such arguments would be a political platform supported by
economic experience, and the major historical trends
of the modern world. Then why has such a platform
not been adopted by the opponents of Afrikaner
nationalism and by the critics of *apartheid*?

Experience in Canada, Belgium and India has shown
that when a political community is divided by sharp
racial or cultural differences which cannot be fused or
merged, there will be certain issues which cannot be
openly or freely handled lest they widen existing cleav-
ages or produce controversies too great to be handled
within the ordinary political system. In South Africa
the great central issues of native affairs became more
intractable as the difference between the two groups
within the European population was emphasized. Any
political party which genuinely advocated a programme
of racial equality under the law would simply destroy
itself. If somehow such a party were to arise and to
strike an open alliance with the leadership of natives,
Indians and coloured men, South Africa would move
into the crisis which the United States endured after
the Dred Scott case. I say this in no spirit of prophecy,
but rather to say that the future of South Africa is so
obscure and opaque that the wise man can do no other
than contemplate it with fearfulness but with a determination not to lose hope.

II

The Delusion of Apartheid

Apartheid is a Dutch or Afrikaans word meaning "apartness", or segregation. Its real meaning is not simple, and its origins are not exclusively Dutch. In South Africa it has its historical roots in Dutch Calvinism and the tribal wars of the nineteenth century. But some of its roots can also be traced to the policies of the British Colonial office. It is not always useful or accurate to distinguish between the English and the Afrikaner in South Africa in racial matters. In Natal, which is the most English of the provinces, the resentment against the Indian population is intense. In 1946 the English-speaking leader of the Labour Party, Walter Madeley, resigned because he opposed the grant of political rights to Indians.

The social, economic and political distinctions which are the structural parts of *apartheid* are in the first place the logical results of the colonial relationship. A relationship of inferiority and superiority was born of the difference between primitiveness and civilization, poverty and wealth, superstition and science. For generations it was implicitly and uncritically assumed that the native population of Africa could be auxiliary to European enterprise and yet continue to live within the social, economic and political system of the rural tribe. This persuasion was contained in a famous and dignified phrase used by Lord Lugard who was a great and conscientious colonial administrator—the Dual Mandate. As a system of governing the natives through their own institutions and at the same time permitting white enterprise to flourish in trade and industrial development the Dual Mandate had an appearance of reasonableness, justice and tolerance. Some of its achievements were remarkable and lasting. In the light of Africa's crisis to-day it is clear that the concepts of segregation and separateness in all their forms and whatever their motivation encouraged the false illusion that white man and black man could live in separate spheres whose margins usefully touched one another, but only in a secondary manner. Race and colour were the visible signs of differences that were primary and permanent. It was this interpretation of race and colour which caused generations of Europeans throughout Africa to accept the view that the only proper environment for the African was the rural tribe. By inference his entry into the social and economic environment created by European enterprise was incidental, impermanent, and even unnatural. In 1922 a Commission appointed by the government of General Smuts declared that the towns were the creation and the special possession of the Europeans, so that the African "should only be allowed to enter urban areas . . . when he is willing to enter and minister to the needs of the white man, and should depart therefrom when he ceases to minister." In Kenya, Rhodesia and South Africa the true meaning of the impact of Europe upon Africa was generally misunderstood. Ideas of separateness in their best forms and their worst conspired to make the governance of the natives an economical way of keeping the peace, and seriously reduced the obligation upon governments and colonists to tend to the economic and political development, the education and welfare of the African population.

If it is wise to speak of error in the policies of the principal metropolitan powers, incomparably their greatest error was the illusion that it was possible to protect and preserve a social order which their own economic activities were destroying. That their beliefs were genuine and often deeply humanitarian does not alter the fact that great populations endured the dislocating pressure of western economic forces while their European rulers failed to bring succour to the growing ruin and chaos in their lives. For all but the discerning few, it was for long generations difficult to see the truth of Arnold Toynbee's description of the entry of the west into the life of the rest of the colonial and backward world. "Future historians will say, I think, that the peak event of the twentieth century was the impact of the western world upon all of the other living societies of the world of that day. They will say of the impact that it was so powerful and so pervasive that it turned the lives of its victims upside down and inside out—affecting the behaviour, outlook, feelings and beliefs of individual men, women and children in an intimate way, touching chords in human souls that are not touched by more external forces, however ponderous and terrifying." It was only after the second World

34

War that it became impossible to ignore the truth that Africa had passed into the stage of crisis, and that men must give earnest thought to the nature of the crisis, and the ways of meeting it.

The forces of modern economic development affect all men no matter what the colour of their skin. The development of Africa in modern times can be more easily understood if it is seen as the result of two movements of migration. The first is the migration of European traders, officials and settlers into Africa together with their skills, investments, equipment and governmental organization. The second is the migration of the African tribesman into the new world created by European enterprise. The chords of human compassion are touched by this record of collapse and renewed struggle, of demoralization and readjustment. The native population did not fall into stagnancy or allow their bodies and spirits to follow the decline of their institutions. While still clinging to the forms of their tribal life they learned the ways of the white man's commerce and industry. Incomparably the outstanding phenomenon of South African history is the struggle of its native population to rise above the atrophy of the tribe, by slowly, painfully and clumsily adapting itself to the functions and activities which western society made available. In South Africa gold and diamonds, trade and manufacture called for the services of black men and white men. At the middle of the twentieth century one-half of the total native population belonged to the working force of the white man's economy. In

1921 there were 500,000 natives in urban areas. In 1936 this number had risen to 1,000,000. A characteristic of all developing modern economies is a radical adjustment of the proportions between rural and urban populations. That manufacture and mining brought 2,000,000 natives to the towns of South Africa is just as natural and inevitable a phenomenon as the urban concentration of 80 per cent of the white population.

In the application of science and technology, in capital investment, mining, industry and commerce there is a power that directs the flow of social events for all men. The degeneration of the tribe was an emancipation of its individuals to become members of the western economic and social system. The breakdown of the tribe was also the genesis of a new society. To the observer standing in a Johannesburg slum it is hard to see emancipation and progress in such a mean and ignoble environment, harder still to see that its inhabitants are not a transient and auxiliary throng whose discomforts and suffering are temporary since their true home is elsewhere in the country with the tribe.

South Africa's urban slums must be regarded as an untidy phenomenon of transition, as a painful stage in the incorporation of a new but indispensable population in the economy of a rapidly growing industrial society. Slums in Johannesburg, Durban and Cape Town are the unsightly camping grounds of men who are laboriously migrating into a new environment in which their rags and filthy shacks are not signs of decline but evidence of their escape from the hopelessness

of their collapsed tribal systems. The truest optimism
in South Africa is in the crowded, disease-ridden and
crime-infested urban locations. They represent the
black man's acceptance of the new life of the western
world, his willingness to endure a harsh schooling and
an unequal apprenticeship in its ways. The dingiest
slum is yet a place of learning. The ragged, underfed
inhabitants are learning many things. Some are adept
in evading the law and defeating the police. Others
learn to read and write, to tend machines, to use money,
to submit to the difficult discipline of punctuality. The
sordidness of their environment hides the great sum of
positive and beneficial achievement, including a share,
however inadequate and disproportionate, in the rising
prosperity and productivity of the country. It hides also
the grim struggle to carry forward the decency and
dignity of the tribe in an unsanitary wilderness where
men build homes out of the industrial rubbish of mine
and factory. They may be likened to the medieval
peasant who settled under the walls of Paris or Augs-
burg, and endured for generations the pains of living in
towns that took little thought how to receive them, and
long delayed the recognition of their citizenship. The
medieval years of great plagues were but spectacular
events in long generations of vileness and overcrowding,
of sickness and hunger. But all the while their residence
was an education in the things which the towns repre-
sented, so that the day came when the descendants of
peasants served in the counting houses of the wealthy,
went forth in great trading ships, rose to high office in

armies, or led their fellows in the conquest of new freedom.

White man and black man have not lived together long enough in the new environment which they are creating together to see that the sum of their similarity and co-operation is each year growing greater than the sum of their differences. Nor have the white communities had time to learn to accept similarity and co-operation lest differences swell and multiply and afflict their society with a sickness that will not heal or that can be cleansed only by tragedy.

That more than three-fourths of the white population of South Africa to-day live in urban areas, and that during a full generation the total natural increase of the rural white population has moved to the towns, are facts that have a convincing meaning. The resources of South Africa can be properly exploited only by concentrating labour and skill in the towns. Conversely, rural South Africa is incapable of building modern prosperity on the soil. The greatest continuous area of sand in the world is South Africa's Kalahari Desert. When experts say that 85 per cent of the country is unfit for cultivation, it is plain that the conventions and laws which inhibit the flow of men and their families to the towns can only become a sentence of poverty and deprivation. Urbanization is the road to progress and prosperity. As incurable rural poverty is the whip that drives South Africa towards ever greater industrialization.

South Africa's racial policies are based on the perverse conviction that the sum of differences between whites and non-whites will always be greater than the sum of their similarities. They do not accept the historical truth that towns in all generations have been centres where culture slowly becomes the common property of all residents, nor do they recognize that in South Africa as in Ancient Greece, the Renaissance or modern America, the growth of new communities proceeds in an atmosphere of long-enduring tension. Meanwhile, life in most urban native locations is precarious, sordid and distressful. One can stand back and let a few phrases and words from the quiet language of the Native Laws Commission of 1948 describe the pains of urbanization for the native population. "The majority of such locations are a menace to the health of the inhabitants . . . disgrace . . . quite unfit for human habitation . . . mere shanties, often nothing more than hovels . . . dark and dirty . . . encumbered with unclean and useless rubbish . . . one could hardly imagine more suitable conditions for the spread of tuberculosis." Indeed, tuberculosis rates in the greater South African towns are amongst the worst in the world. Life expectancy in the non-white population is low, as it was in the slums of most European towns before the great modern improvements in sanitation, medicine and nutrition. Even in salubrious Cape Town amongst the relatively more advanced coloured people the life expectancy of a coloured man is full twenty years less than that of his white neighbour. Undernourishment and malnutrition afflict a high proportion of the non-

European population. They are a major cause of the inertia, laziness and fecklessness which inexperienced observers regard as inborn racial characteristics. South Africa's genial sun and healthy climate are a subsidy which partially hides the neglect of its municipalities, and a mercifulness without which the slums of Cape Town and Johannesburg would go beyond the worst suffering of the most distressful period of the Middle Ages. By the side of filth, disease and poverty there is also criminality and immorality. Elements of the population who are unmannerly and unsightly by day, criminal and dangerous by night, explain why there is each year a significant increase in crime. The defects of the native urban population are more obvious than their aptitudes. It requires experience and impartiality to see that there is also a great sum of courage, enlightenment and decency. When men are uninformed or unsympathetic they naturally analyse the native urban populations by a catalogue of their defects and by the unpleasant manifestations of their disorganized entry into the European economy. They are also easily led to the view that the correction of abuse is essentially a task for the police, and that the natives are an alien population living in an environment that is unnatural and unfitting for them. Most significant is the persuasion that the proper reforms of the evils of native urban life must be found in restraint, separation and even exclusion. Crime and turbulence seem to be the mark of the native who attempts to take on the alien culture of the white man's world. Twentieth-century South Africa has not exactly rediscovered the noble savage of the eighteenth century. But it has come to the conclusion that goodness is more easily found in the natives who cling to their own culture and live in their own separate environment.

There is already a considerable body of writing which exposes the discriminatory and oppressive character of the racial policies of South Africa. An image has been created of a harsh and vindictive generation of men who are engaged in fastening a selfish and dictatorial regime upon their fellow men. (The unfriendly analysis of *apartheid* has become good sport, and is an easy road to editorial popularity) *Apartheid* is no subject for mockery or facile comment. It is very grim, very important, very difficult. Of the men in South Africa who support it some are uninformed and deeply prejudiced; still others are angry or frightened; many feel helpless or bewildered; selfishness and indifference are common. These attitudes are easily discernible amongst both English and Afrikaans-speaking sections of the population. There is, however, a gross and dangerous error in not recognizing that the best of the advocates of *apartheid* are men of personal worthiness, with genuinely conscientious and moral spirits. This concession is not in conflict with the opposite admission that there exists in the present government an ugly and sinister self-righteousness which seems prepared to sacrifice the liberty and comity of a democratic society in order to attain the harsh ends of an imperious racial nationalism. Yet it is still wrong to believe that a body of ungenerous and selfish motives is all that sustains the doctrines of *apartheid*.

The major pronouncements on racial policy are often remarkable for their frank avowal of the inequities and deficiencies from which the native population suffers. The best of them are free of the traditional dismissal of the natives as incorrigibly backward. Scholarship in this field is often objective and undistorted. The more scholarly proponents of *apartheid* are emphatically not ignorant or ruthless men. Their work shows a penetrating and detailed awareness of facts and figures. It is important to know indeed how much earlier ignorance and indifference have been replaced by knowledge and awareness. It is possible to gather together out of their writings much of the evidence on which the opposition to *apartheid* is founded. *Apartheid* has within it the basis for re-education and a new recognition of the realities of South African life.

It is easy to cull the literature of *apartheid* and bring forth passages which proclaim, not exclusion and denial, but the creation of fuller opportunities and liberties for the natives. It is with real sincerity that many men feel that new and worthy horizons can be opened for the natives. These attitudes explain the pain and indignation which South Africans sometimes show when their policies are assailed in the foreign press or the United Nations. There is no deliberate hypocrisy in the frequent statement that *apartheid* is first of all a movement of emancipation and reform. Even as the Afrikaner has struggled to maintain his language and culture, and win freedom and dignity in his own land, so it surely is a Christian and honourable purpose to lead the native to a condition where he can maintain his own language and develop his own culture, build his own institutions, and above all escape from his unhappy and unequal position in an alien society. In his own homeland, separate from the world of the white man, there will be no passes or curfew, no social indignity, no nightly routine of police raids and arrests. *Apartheid* thus becomes a glowing picture of release and advancement, which are both of them the fruit of the white man's wisdom and self-sacrifice.

Once it is assumed that the white and non-white populations are racially and culturally incompatible it is logical and statesmanlike to express this fact in a separation of the races. To the few extreme theoreticians of the political science of *apartheid* this disengagement of white and non-white should be complete in every way, however great the cost and discomfort to the white population. The white population must place the purity of its race and culture above material self-interest, and endure great sacrifices to preserve its separate identity. Such statements give an apparent sense of freshness and excitement. That they contrast with the often muffled, ambiguous and evasive pronouncements of the political opponents of the Nationalist Party is one explanation of the electoral success of the Nationalist Party. They draw a picture of a proud people facing a difficult future with boldness and enterprise and justice. As long as white and black live together in their present unnatural intimacy the white man is forced to take unchristian steps to protect his race and culture. Therefore, it is moral and Christian and statesmanlike for the races to be separated so that each may enjoy his own. To deny the rights of civilization to the African would indeed be oppressive and lead to hatred and strife. The decision that the black man be excluded from the life of the white man is balanced and justified by another decision which permits the black man to develop a life of his own along the freest and most generous lines.

In the solemn and conscientious atmosphere of pulpit and library the legislation of *apartheid* represents a difficult period of transition and adjustment which all men must courageously endure before the new order can be established. Thus the laws of *apartheid* are transformed into sacrifice and deprivation which the European community inflicts upon itself in order to yield the rights of civilization to all men, black and white. What seems in Delhi or London to be oppression becomes an act of emancipation; what seems rejection is a gateway to opportunity. As Prime Minister Strydom advised the native population: "You must learn to develop your own areas so that your homeland can become prosperous. You must learn to govern yourselves in your own areas. You must learn to become your own traders, builders, carpenters, doctors, welfare workers and so forth. This is a separate development and must be based on your own way of life. In all respects you must learn to make your own communities self-sufficient."

Because *apartheid* has diverse origins it means different things to different people. Hypocrisy and selfishness combine with idealism to give it purchase on the minds of men. It is easy to criticize the racial laws of South Africa on humanitarian or historical grounds. It is not difficult to show that those whose advocacy is truly high-minded have simply abolished the real world about them, and have created a paradise without history and in defiance of economics. For the thoughtful man it is still important to understand how men who are sincere in their Christian beliefs and staunch defenders of their own liberties can become identified with policies of discrimination and restriction.

White South Africans feel insecure and are afraid. In this they are akin to Frenchmen in Algeria or Jews in Israel. To borrow a term from nuclear physics, the problem is partly one of critical mass. If the whites of South Africa were a small and scattered community, such as the British were in India, or the Gold Coast, their lack of numbers and compactness would have a compelling influence on political development, however great their reluctance. If on the other hand they enjoyed the numerical preponderance of white Americans, concessions would be easier because security would be greater. The decision of the United States Supreme Court against racial discrimination in education was more than a statement of principle. It was also a manifestation of security. Tolerance does not flourish easily in an atmosphere of fear and insecurity. White South Africa, with a total population of nearly 2,500,000 is large enough and compact enough to have a strong feeling of corporateness. Their status as a self-governing state is as meaningful to South Africans as it is to Canadians or New Zealanders. They know that in a modern state citizenship is more than suffrage, and cannot be conferred merely by document or decree. Citizenship has little real meaning unless it is supported by a foundation of education and skills, by respect for law and the knowledge that the moral principles of integrity and incorruptibility are practical requirements for orderly and civilized government. These are some of the reasons why the white community is proud and jealous of its political and cultural achievements, and why also it is afraid of the numbers, the inexperience, and the disorderliness of the natives. It is true that the historical and inescapable challenge of every plural or multi-racial society is to develop a larger patriotism in which differences of race, language and creed are subordinated to the major purpose of social harmony, political stability, economic progress, and human dignity. It is also true that it is supremely difficult, and for most ordinary men impossible, to see how such orderliness and coherence can be built out of such a wilderness of broken tribes, superstition, ignorance and sloth as they see about them. In their society, with its towns and factories and schools and government, white South Africans have a possession which they feel they have won with their blood and their courage, with their money and their labour. Modern South Africa is their creation, and only they can ensure its survival and progress.

46

It is impossible to escape a sense of helplessness in the face of these problems. Whoever discusses them is constantly tempted to lay aside his pen in a spirit of humility and compassion. Yet as there must be action so must there first be thought. Men are made less helpless as they understand more, and scholarship cannot lay down its duty of statesmanship. The scholar cannot escape the obligation of criticism and evaluation. Some of his language must be direct. *His criticism begins* —

In its various forms *apartheid* is a transfer of the responsibilities of the living world to a dream world of solved problems. It is the substitution of a wishful simplicity for a real complexity. The basic premise of *apartheid* is that the natives can seek no remedies and gain no citizenship within white society, but only within their own segregated society. It is at this critical point that the remarkably well-written documents issued by the South African Bureau of Racial Affairs step from fact into make-believe, using a dexterous logic to brush aside history and economics. Their phrases throb and glow with the justice and the enlightenment that will mark the condition of all men in the clean, logical world of racial separation. Their pages are now free of feelings of guilt and frustration. The writers are at peace with their own conscience and in harmony with world opinion. There is no awareness in the architects of *apartheid* that out of fact and fancy they have ingeniously contrived a mental toy, operating outside history and economics. They do indeed invoke economic and political principles, but they are the principles of a nonexistent world, so that their scholarship becomes spurious and their logic a deception. Yet these solemn treatises on race politics, properly construed, are an excellent measure of the bafflement and complexity of South African life. By inversion they are avowals of pessimism, frustration and even guilt. Under the guise of hope and deliverance the formula of *apartheid* is a creed of despair and a flight from the fearfulness of the real problem. In the old days of native wars Voortrekkers drew their wagons into a circle or laager. Within its protection men defended themselves against the impis of the Zulus or the Matabele. To-day their descendants seek to retreat within a new laager made up of laws and restraints as if they could thereby be protected against the turmoil of a multi-racial society. In their statements when they mean them most sincerely, there is both confession and absolution. There is the confession that the natives cannot be indefinitely denied the privileges of modern life. There is a self-administered absolution of guilt in the promise that these privileges can be theirs. They cannot gain them at the expense of the white man by swamping him with the vote or depressing his standard of living by their competition. But they can achieve them in their own separate areas. This is the higher purpose of *apartheid*.

Such generosity is illusion, and such liberality is fantasy. It is a vision of a false and unattainable utopia imposed upon a native population that does not aspire to it.

The moment will certainly come when a competent

study of the policy of developing separate native economic and industrial systems will reveal the shocking balance sheet of impossible expense, inefficiency and social waste which must be the result of trying to herd men into separate areas of life and labour.[1]

The real lines that are drawn by *apartheid* are not drawn between two acceptable spheres of settlement and opportunity. Unhappily they are lines drawn in the mind and the heart, cut deeply by the hatred of the black man for the police, by the resentment of parents who cannot educate their children, by the frustration of men who move daily to and fro between squalor at home and meniality at work, by the dangerous anger of native leaders whose westernized minds can fully measure the indignity and deprivation which are inflicted upon them, by the slow mounting of a conviction that *apartheid* is a frontier of conflict where differences can be resolved only through resistance, violence and sabotage. In the concrete language of economics and politics *apartheid* is actually a system in which the power of the state is used to maintain the economic and political supremacy of the white community over a population of approximately ten million Africans, Indians and coloured men. The segregation laws are an embargo upon the development of the non-European population. In its extreme form *apartheid* punishes the native for his past by robbing him of the future. These laws seek to imprison the population within its own

[1] Since these words were written the Tomlinson Report has substantially drawn up this balance sheet.

backwardness, and set up blockades against the flow of experience, skills, and amenities on which modern progress is based. In South Africa there is the most marked trend towards what Thomas Jefferson called an elective despotism. The European population lives under a liberal constitution and within a democratic framework which are the equivalent of those in Canada or Australia. But the rest of the population lives largely outside the constitution and under a growing body of laws and administrative decisions designed to impose upon them a separate status and a separate function in the life of the State.

South Africa is a democracy built upon subject peoples. It is a system of free enterprise built upon the labour of unfree and subordinate men. South Africa's critics have sometimes been intemperate in using epithets taken from totalitarian societies. It is easy to forget that some of the unfreedom and inequality has deep and obstinate roots in long centuries of history. The proper words to use of a society which contains the opposites of freedom and unfreedom, of equality and inequality, are difficult to find. In an earlier generation A. V. Dicey contrasted the Rule of Law, as a characteristic of British political development, with an opposite regime in which government or its agents could exercise "wide, arbitrary or discretionary powers of constraint." From the point of view of a Natal Indian who cannot vote, an African who cannot become a skilled craftsman, or an educated coloured man who cannot stand for Parliament, the Rule of Law in South Africa is not complete, democracy is qualified, and free enterprise is limited. For the bulk of its population South Africa is a police state. It is not possible in the modern world to elevate the few by depressing the many. When men cannot work in freedom, or when unequal groups cannot grow towards greater equality, they become prisoners of one another, bound by the same fears and exposed to the same dangers. Since the non-European population is an intimate part of the total population, the regime of arbitrary police action and statutory offences restricts the ordinary rule of law for all citizens.

In the United States the amendments to the Constitution and the judicial interpretations by the Supreme Court have gradually removed or diminished special economic or political limitations upon individuals or groups of individuals. In law, if not always in practice, the results are binding upon legislatures, administrations and courts. In South Africa the tendency for many years has been to develop a special system of laws applicable only to the native population. The Ministry of Native Affairs can rule by proclamation against which no appeal to any court of law is possible. Different statutes specifically define a large number of offences of which only a native can be guilty. The Native Administration Act and the much amended Riotous Assemblies Act give the police very wide powers to control the activities of individuals and organizations. The principle of courts that administer the same law equally to all men is fully applicable only to the European community.

To a Zulu or Basuto labourer in an industrial community like Johannesburg the term police state has an added meaning. The laws often lead to harsh police action and summary court procedures which would produce a major scandal if applied to even the worst elements of the European population. Between four and five per cent of the total native population is arrested each year for statutory offences such as failing to show a pass or breaking the strict curfew laws. There is evidence to indicate that between fifteen and twenty per cent of the adult male population in the urban areas is arrested by the police each year.

The catalogue is long of laws which divide race from race and confine men in separate compartments. To explain and analyse them fully is a lengthy and complicated task. The Nationalist Party has declared a war of the laws of Parliament against the laws of economics and against the new rules which the modern world is struggling to apply to its racial affairs. The Prohibition of Mixed Marriages Act makes a crime of marriage between a white man and a person of colour. The Population Registration Act enjoins the compilation of a national register according to race with the intention of confining the present population and its descendants within fixed racial compartments. The Native Labour Act and the Industrial Conciliation Amendment Act undertake to separate natives from Europeans in the trade union movement, and to confine native labour to categories of less skill and lower pay. The prohibition of strikes by natives, the ban upon direct collective bargaining, and the provision that any breach of contract is a criminal offence shackle and confine native workers in a fashion for which parallels can be found only in the earliest stages of the European industrial revolution.

The Bantu Education Act is presented as a notable widening of opportunity for the natives. In the language of the Minister for Native Affairs "all doors are open", and the native can be educated "to serve his community in all respects." In the much less tidy world of racial commingling and interdependence the Bantu Education Act is a more sinister instrument. Its real intention is to arrest the rise of the native population in the western world, and to confine him to a lowly and menial position within it. The late Principal Davie of the University of Cape Town was a sturdy man, and a South African amongst South Africans. In his words, the intention of the Bantu Education Act is to "establish and perpetuate an inferior status in relation to the European." Education aims to prepare the native child for a service "which is primarily that of servant of the Europeans and secondly one which carries with it no promise of advancement towards the eventual social and political status which he covets . . ." Since a great and growing proportion of the native population must live and work in the European areas the Act sets up a total contradiction between what is promised in the native community and denied in the European community, as if the same men can be both bound and unbound according to where they happen to be. Despite its promises the Act reaffirms the white man's monopoly of the technical knowledge and managerial experience through which he controls the economy. It revives the familiar argument of the first generation of the industrial revolution in Great Britain that the education of the poor illiterate masses makes them less fitted for their tasks and less content with their appointed station. Education along western lines is a disservice to the natives and to the nation.

A deeper contradiction reveals the doctrinaire and unrealistic nature of much of the thought and legislation of *apartheid*. To live and work in a European community is to grow in understanding and competence. Almost every service the natives perform, even the act of buying shoes or stealing automobile tyres, becomes obscurely and infinitesimally a step in western education. As science and technology are further invoked to increase the nation's productivity, no part of the nation's labour force, not even the lowliest, can be artificially segregated in a special area of ignorance and incompetence.

The whole myth of a separate native culture collapses when it is recognized that, for the African, progress and emancipation depend upon an escape from the tribe and a deeper entry into the life of the West. At its best and strongest, native leadership aspires to abandon the past and seek a future in the western world. Its goals are education, opportunity and advancement in the environment created by European enterprise. In far-off East Africa the Mau Mau tragedy shows that the African has nothing to resuscitate in protest against the white man except tribalism, no tradition to invoke higher or more dignified than the cruel sanctions of witchcraft and barbarism. On the face of the earth there are few non-western peoples who depend more than the African upon the west for everything that can be called advancement and progress.

The sum of segregation laws are an effort to prevent failure in a white man and success in a black man. The horizontal and vertical separation of white and non-white is carried forward by the controversial Group Areas Act and the Native Resettlement Act. The first Act aims to create separate zones of habitation in the urban areas for coloured men, natives, Indians and Europeans. The second seeks to remove all natives from the western areas of Johannesburg and relocate them in separate areas on the far outskirts of Africa's greatest industrial community. Provided the basic assumptions of racial and cultural separateness are accepted, these acts once again have admirable qualities of orderliness and reform. They disengage communities whose commingling causes provocation and discord. They will flush out the sordid slums from the major urban centres, and aid the work of the police in the more compact and homogeneous racial communities. These facts, which must not lightly be dismissed, explain the tacit consent with which these laws are received throughout much of the European population of South Africa. Even a brief residence in Johannesburg makes men hungry for something to be done to end the shame and disorder and danger of its slums. But genuine reform is more than the removal of human bodies and arbitrarily making them wards of the police. The truth about these acts is that they are an attack upon the assimilative tendencies of urban life. They strike at the hope for which the meanest hovel stood, and block the daily effort of men to find some lodgement in the only environment in which they could earn their nourishment. They are a confiscation of the tiny worlds of little freedoms and opportunities which humble folk were nurturing for themselves and their children. More fundamentally these acts are major restraints upon individualism and the acquisition and use of private property. Johannesburg's new distant locations are an enforced assemblage of men and women into groups to which coercion and control can be swiftly applied. They are an arbitrary creation of communities for purposes of supervision and discipline. The concept of urban locations as a dormitory for a cheap labour force imposes severe disabilities on both industry and labour. It puts a premium on inefficiency, and instability. It depresses earnings and production. This in turn continues the cycle of malnutrition, insecurity and crime. It is even an endorsement of the prostitution, drunkenness, juvenile delinquency and viciousness which persuade even thoughtful white men that a harsh police regime is the only governance the natives can understand.

In a generation less confused by some of the economic and social analysis of the nineteenth century, it is becoming plainer that democratic freedoms are fuller and more meaningful where men are free to improve their economic status and spend their earnings on the goods of their choice. Far more significant at this moment than the laws which restrict rights of political representation and suffrage are the laws and restraints which limit the power of the non-European to earn and his right to acquire and use property. In the free market economy of the western world, earning power and property in the broadest sense are indispensable to individual prestige and influence. To be able to earn more and to buy a widening range of goods and services is in itself an important extension of freedom. At the core of a healthy western democracy there is an area, relatively free of political control, where skills and shillings, industriousness and spending power are the ballots which the man who works and consumes casts in a daily plebiscite where his influence is not limited by his race or the colour of his skin. At its best this is a wide area, "detoxicated" of organized political and statutory control, in which men and groups have considerable initiative in working out the conditions of their economic and social co-operation. The economic progress of the African is a process which enlarges his liberty, tempers the impact of racial discrimination and political arbitrariness. To the extent that the African cannot enter this area of free action he becomes a bondsman, herded into labour camps and condemned to a stagnant and hopeless meniality.

Unusual confidence in the democratic process is required to see that such a zone of freedom for all can exist in a multi-racial society composed of groups on uneven levels of culture. It is the strongest proof of the pessimistic and the authoritatian political philosophy of *apartheid* that it runs rigid and statutory frontiers through the very area which in Great Britain, the United States and Canada are generously open for private initiative, voluntary association, or local government.

Long ago Alexis de Tocqueville noticed the rôle played by private, spontaneous and voluntary effort on the raw and formative American frontier. On the frontier, men experimented with the methods and institutions which would enable them to achieve the co-operativeness and stability of settled communities. The new communities were an area in which men grew in knowledge of one another in their daily association and by methods that were spontaneous, experimental and expedient. They worked out the techniques and institutions of which the fruit was political harmony, social improvement and economic co-operation. In South Africa, however, where the relations between different groups are totally governed by a body of imperative laws passed by a central authority, democracy is weakened in a most vital area. It is the area in which tolerant men explain their minds, and where new ideas and institutions are born. It is an area of incubation. It is not merely a zone of material contact and commercial exchange, but also of spiritual creativeness and intellectual fertility. These are fruitful areas where impulses and discoveries are possible that are unattainable by legislatures and courts. One function of the laws of a democratic society is to protect the vitality and freedom of these areas of personal initiative and of voluntary and spontaneous effort. Otherwise they become barren, and the healthy self-governance of the many is surrendered to political parties, government departments, and statutes. One of the indispensable conditions of a thriving and resourceful democracy is that there must be activities and relationships for which the state and organized political power do not lay down the rules of conduct or define the canons of success. Where legislatures and courts encroach too severely upon the realm where ideas like individualism, personal initiative, voluntary association acquire their full meaning and stature, by maintaining privileges of race, imposing restrictions on education and employment, or entrenching the few at the expense of the many, they create a desert of economic frustration, political sterility and social disruption. The guardians of the desert are the police. Of all the causes for fear in modern South Africa this desert is the greatest.

In later generations historians may well assert that the worst consequence of this period of racialism was that it permitted old institutions to collapse, and yet prevented the evolution in an atmosphere of co-operation and consent of new institutions and relationships to meet the requirements of rapid economic and social change in a multi-racial society.

III

Time for Decision

IN THE thought and action of *apartheid* there is undeniably an absolutist quality which leads the state to take increasing possession of every individual, according to race, colour, language, and to guide each into his proper segregated compartment. The maintenance of political power tends increasingly to become the primary issue in the state. In a still more serious fashion economic, social and educational problems become first of all political issues, decided by statutes administered by magistrates and police. The life of the state is exposed to the danger of degenerating into a pervasive struggle for political power, in which racial hatred and social violence feed upon tension and frustration. A premium is placed upon struggle and conflict rather than co-operation. If South Africa has set its foot on the road to increasing authoritarianism, it also makes more likely an ultimate and awesome battle of the non-European population against the political domination of the whites.

These are such serious considerations that they must be fully explained, and where necessary honestly qualified or even contradicted. In a psychological sense a situation is being created in which disagreement with the racial and cultural policies of the Nationalist party is unpatriotic. Under the Suppression of Communism Act overt action against these policies may even become

TREASON

seditious and treasonable, since it is legally in the power of the Minister to label an act as communist and to apply the severe sanctions of the law to the accused individual.

The rise of political freedom and toleration in the western world from the seventeenth century onwards was marked by a progressive reduction in the number of attitudes or acts which could be branded and punished as seditious, treasonable or heretical. The story of political and religious freedom in Great Britain and North America in the past century is most quickly told by noting the extreme rareness of the trial and punishment of acts of sedition or treason or heresy. Whenever in the course of human history an act can be loaded with the awful gravamen of both treason and heresy, liberty and tolerance are in mortal danger. The nature of militant communism in modern Russia is such that it has re-established the fearful bond between treason and heresy. Anybody familiar with the passionate episodes of Calvinist persecution or the Inquisition has little difficulty in understanding the purges, confessions, recantations and penalties of the treason trials in Russia which claims the millennial powers of Providence, and imposes upon its citizens the twin obligation of stern patriotism and rigid orthodoxy.

It would be misleading and unfair to declare that the discipline and uniformity to which the more militant forms of Afrikaner nationalism and racialism aspire, show a clear trend back to the political and doctrinal discipline of early Calvinism. It would be offensive not to be clear about the sturdy spirit of freedom of the Afrikaner people, or to forget that at his best the Afrikaner liberal, in Carl Becker's witty phrase, has few peers and no equals. Yet it is true that the position of the Afrikaner liberal to-day, even in the universities, is more lonely and exposed than it was a generation ago. No reflective observer can fail to note the seventeenth-century voices in the politically powerful Dutch Reformed Church who proclaim that the State of the Afrikaner people and its authority are the creation of God. A government minister actually asserted that the effort to pack the Senate in order to secure the two-thirds majority necessary to override the Constitution was justifiable on both political and religious grounds. "We are taking this step," he said, "because we are Calvinists who believe God is sovereign and that sovereignty is delegated to the lawful rulers of the land." The concept of indivisible power in a state specifically charged with the preservation of racial purity and ascendancy is hospitable to authoritarian procedures. Opposition based on the purpose of giving natives, Indians and coloured men a greater share in the total life of the State is also more likely to become seditious and heretical if it alters a political community ordered by God himself. It is when a society lives in the shadow of danger, or passes into a period of deep unrest and disquietude, that the political faith by which it is guided is of the greatest moment. The raging controversy over the South African Constitution is most illuminating. The effort of the

Nationalist government to deprive the coloured population of the Cape Province of their place on the common voters roll, collides with one of the entrenched clauses of the Constitution. The Nationalist government is determined to secure the two-thirds majority of the two Houses of Parliament in single session which is necessary to amend the Constitution. The Separate Representation of Voters Act passed by both houses of Parliament was declared unconstitutional by the courts. A controversy of great intensity arose concerning the nature of the Constitution. Was it more like the British Constitution under which the sovereignty of Parliament is virtually unqualified? Or was it more like the American Constitution which is binding on the Legislature and authorizes independent interpretation by the Supreme Court? In the theory of constitutional law powerful arguments can be marshalled to support either point of view. In the condition of modern South Africa the issue has become a wider one. At least in the minds of a militant wing of the Nationalist party the appropriateness of parliamentary government itself is in question.

There are three principal arguments advanced against the existing forms and procedures of constitutional parliamentary government. Of these only the third has any real significance. The first argument is historical. It is based on the assertion with which serious historians cannot agree, that the political organization of the two Boer Republics was evolving away from British practice. The second argument is an emotional and patriotic deduction from the first. It is an expression of anti-

British sentiment. Patriotically extreme Afrikaner nationalism feels a desire to be purged of constitutional principles that were formulated, and political decisions that were reached in the period of so-called British domination. The third argument is by far the most serious. It is the child of *apartheid*.

A small white community is surrounded by a numerous and backward native population which threatens its security, its culture, its standard of living, its racial purity, and its political dominance. A compact and vocal Indian population has exposed the domestic life of South Africa to foreign diplomatic and economic pressure. There is even a distant military threat in the power vacuum which exists in the Indian Ocean. The white population must therefore close its ranks. It must assemble its physical and political power. Political life must become a fortress manned by resolute men who will defend the integrity of white civilization. The nation does not face a temporary emergency which will pass. It faces a crisis continuing through the generations which cannot be met by the debates, delays and compromises of parliamentary government based on a two-party system. For the safety and welfare of the entire white community it is essential that non-European affairs be expelled from ordinary political life. Certainly the coloured population cannot have an entrenched position in the constitution, nor an independent voice through the suffrage. In this context the efforts to override the constitution and to destroy the power of the courts to uphold the constitution, flow directly from the conviction that in racial affairs there is only one correct policy. The party which upholds such a policy has a moral and historic right to prevail over all others. Discipline, solidarity, racial purity, the comradeship of right-thinking men—these are familiar words in our generation. That they have currency in the great South African debate is yet another reminder of the authoritarianism which has arisen within South African political life.

The battle over the constitution has been won by the Nationalist government. The Senate has been packed and has been made into the docile instrument of the Nationalist party. It seems safe to say that the special position of the Constitution has been destroyed, though at the time of going to press the validity of the new Senate is itself being tested in the Courts. In law there seems little opposition left to the will of the Nationalist majority in Parliament. But there is another and greater battle to be fought.

In South Africa the laws of Parliament are at war with the laws of economics. *Apartheid* is at variance with many of the essential requirements of a growing modern industrial society. In the modern world it is a dissipation of wealth not to use the energies and skills of the whole population, or to inhibit the full development of the productive powers of any class in the population. Economic development and the more effective utilization of the native labour force are inseparable. The effort to extrude the native, or to hold him down to an inferior status condemns the whole of society, European and non-European, to a lesser economic development than is attainable. The economic growth of South Africa in modern times is based upon the exploitation of exceptional sources of wealth such as diamonds, gold, coal and uranium. From the special point of view of the economist, South Africa's ten million non-Europeans are also a windfall, a great natural resource. They are immigrants who do not have to immigrate. They are a mine of energy and potential skill. In a modern world where science and technology establish new horizons of economic development South Africa actually suffers from under-population and a serious shortage of trained and skilled workers. The evidence is very clear that a population of two and a half million Europeans is an inadequate pool from which to draw the country's skilled manpower. In other progressive industrial societies the demand for a greater and higher degree of education and training increases with each generation. In some countries like the United States a shortage of trained and skilled manpower may already be more serious than a shortage of capital. Reliable statistics show that even as the standard of living of the native has greatly improved so also have important advances been made in his educational attainments. In these things South Africa compares very advantageously with any other British territory in Africa. The great sinning of *apartheid* is its refusal to incorporate these facts into the logic and purpose of economic and political life. The refusal to accept the meaning and great promise of these advances breeds frustration and anger.

The perverse economics of *apartheid* sees alien invaders instead of needed immigrants, and over-population where there is really under-population. It does not realize that backwardness is a form of remediable underdevelopment. It does not recognize that in spite of differences of race and cultural attainments the confluence and congruency of economic interests between European and non-European are greater than conflict and competition. The frustration of the many is the frustration of all.

HIST. EX. There is danger in citing examples from the economic and social history of older and racially different societies. Yet one secret of the great social stability of Great Britain or the United States which seemed so unlikely in the age of the Chartists and the Communist Manifesto was the recognition in national legislation and economic practice that an expanding use of the benefits of income and property by all sections of society are the indispensable pillars of prosperity and social peace. Great Britain and the United States, each in its own way, proceeded in the nineteenth and twentieth centuries to prove that the extension of political freedom and economic opportunity was possible without revolution, and without the bloody settlement of insoluble contradictions predicted by Marx and Engels. The full story has not yet been told of the interaction of science and technology, laws and judicial decisions, social conscience and scholarship, which has created the liberal economic democracies of Great Britain and America. Yet incomparably the best explanation of the

67

growth, the stability and the hope of the greater western democracies is their ability to increase the sum of material satisfaction and dignity for men of the most diverse creeds and origins by a progressive abandonment of restraints and discrimination, and a corresponding agreement that no man can be effective as a citizen or a worker if by some special law or prejudice he is prevented from developing the powers of his body and his mind. The economist can state this very simply. The population of South Africa is twelve and a half million. Of these about ten million are inefficient, unskilled and uneducated. In a modern society these are serious handicaps, which stand in the way of fully exploiting the great mineral wealth of the country, of conserving its precious water, of increasing its food production, of attracting more investment capital, and above all of permitting an expanding prosperity to help solve the country's great social problems.

In South Africa's economic system the cheap labour of unskilled men is used in place of adequate investment, and of well-paid and well-trained workers. The emphasis is upon cheapness and quantity rather than upon productivity and quality. One of the most emphatic impressions reached by a competent observer of native labour is its excessive wastefulness. It is wasteful because it is ignorant and untrained. It is wasteful because it is often ill-nourished. Arrests and imprisonment subtract countless working days from the nation's labour force. The system of migratory labour causes lengthy absences, and a costly turnover of workers. A growing spirit of resentment and sullenness undermines incentive and ambition.

Of what economists call the net geographic money product of the Union the share of the native population in 1951–2 was approximately 14 per cent. Before the war in 1938 the European population received 80 per cent of the national income. These figures are sometimes used as a measure of the economic exploitation of the natives by the Europeans. The *per capita* income of the Union's native population is actually very much higher than in any other African territory. The average native in the Union has at least three times the income of the average native in Kenya, and the rise in his standard of living is much faster. These figures, however, are far more meaningful as a measure of the damage done to the natives and the whole economy by the combined effects of backwardness and discrimination. Amongst African territories the productivity of the Union is most impressive. For 1951–2 the net national income is given as £1,244,800,000. But in the same year Canada had a net national income of £5,743,000,000. It is a simple calculation to prove that South Africa with four-fifths of the Canadian population produces only 21.7 per cent of Canada's national income.

That the laws of economics and the requirements of industrial efficiency are at war with the laws of Parliament is a notable cause for hope. By the side of the liberal spirits in politics and intellectual life, there exists a virtual fifth column of engineers, economists, industrialists, and business men. They are not organized and

HOPE *

have no leadership. Their actions are often irresolute and expedient. Their power is less in themselves than in the coercion implicitly exercised by investments, science, technology and the market place. Whatever their politics or timidity, their faces are perforce set against waste, inefficiency, and unproductivity.

Not South Africa alone, but most of Africa south of the Sahara, has suffered since the second World War from a chronic labour shortage. This fact alone exposes the grim nonsense of the Alice in Wonderland economics of *apartheid*. At the very moment that the theorists of racial separation are solemnly debating the new self-sufficient communities that must arise in the separate native areas, well-paid agents of the mining companies are at work night and day to pump the able-bodied native male population into the industrial areas. It has been estimated that by 1959 the gold mining industry alone will require 80,000 additional native workers. Industrial management itself has opened breaches which permit native labour to enter semi-skilled occupations and to earn higher wages.

There are a number of frontiers across which natives are quietly drifting into more skilled and better paid occupations. The evidence is steadily mounting that behind a continuing barrage of speeches and gestures the Nationalist government itself is yielding to economic pressure. Even in the rural areas, which are the stronghold of *apartheid*, the average wages in cash and kind of native workers rose by about 16 per cent between 1947 and 1952. Every step forward in mechanized and scien-

70

tific farming also increases the demand for greater competence on the part of native farm labour. Even in government service it has been impossible to prevent natives from moving into positions where greater skill and responsibility are required. Foreign opinion, it is obvious, must not fall into the trap of believing that the propaganda and laws of the Nationalist government tell the whole story. South Africa is a land of contradictions. By the side of the rivalry of the races there is an even more fundamental struggle between the forces of separation, and the opposite forces of integration. The process of investment, industrialization and urbanization are processes of integration and amalgamation. In Great Britain what Disraeli once called the two nations were ultimately fused into one by the integrating power of technology, social conscience and economic understanding.

Economic wisdom and self-interest favour a fuller use of all South Africa's manpower, all its water, all its land. All natural resources should be more fully used. The time has come when South Africa can no longer allow the inefficient husbandry of ignorant men to deplete and destroy the fertility of the native reserves. The total South African economy needs the efficient use of both natives and the land on which they live. The economic principles of *apartheid* are bad simply because they are upside down. By trying to herd the native population back into separate economic and political areas the Nationalist government is in effect allying itself with the primitive and backward components of native life,

with those customs and practices which are the first
cause of poverty and stagnation. It is an unseemly
marriage between white stupidity and black incompetence which can only breed poverty and despair. The
unhappy offspring cannot be segregated; for it is the
quality of unhappiness that it afflicts the whole society
in which it exists. If a nation cannot be half-slave and
half-free, it cannot be half-poor and half-rich. The
poverty of the natives and of their land is in the long
run a subtraction from the wealth available to all. The
entry of the capital and the skill of the West into the
backward native areas, and the entry of the backward
native population into the service of western capital
and skills are two phases of the same favourable process
of growth and development.

Apartheid is not the creation of the white man alone.
The native tribe is itself a special form of isolation. The
most effective ally of the white man's segregation
policies is the hold of tribalism on the habits and beliefs
of a considerable proportion of the native population.
In a difficult and painful age it is understandable that
these confused men should seek escape and security in
tribal life, and in the separate tribal areas which still
remain to them. But such security is illusory and such
escape ineffective. One explanation of the tangled and
intractable appearance of economic and political problems in South Africa is that the native population is in
conflict with itself. Those who have not entirely broken
away from the life of the tribe continue to shuttle between incompatible worlds of cash and subsistence. In

the town they are refugees from the poverty of the reserves; in the reserves they are refugees from the indignity of the town. They are the victims of insecurity wherever they are, undernourished in one place and underprivileged in another. Their life is an alternation between stagnation and frustration. They embrace a broken past, because they cannot see a better future.

In a debate which has become worldwide men have their choice between widely divergent predictions of what the future holds for South Africa. In gross terms there seem to be two roads. Through the influence of economic necessity and a recognition of the major trends in the modern world away from discrimination, racial prejudice and colonialism, the first road leads to greater liberalism and co-operation. The second road leads from resentment to strife, and from strife probably to disaster. On the most various grounds it seems safe to predict that the policy of *apartheid* can lead to greater tyranny, but it cannot lead to security or stability. The greater its severity the swifter may be the journey to tragedy.

Physically, the non-European population is naked and helpless before the power of police and heavily armed riot squads. But in its resentment there is a force beyond the reach of physical armament. The evidence of a hardening temper in the entire non-European population suggests a grim race between the forces of integration and the forces of disintegration and social collapse. It is already possible to speak of a groundswell of discontent and resentment in the entire non-European

population of natives, Indians and coloured men. Much
of it is still unorganized and incoherent. AND There is, however, a group that must be watched with the closest
attention. It is the group of those natives who are fully
westernized or so largely westernized that they have
no real roots in tribal life and custom. These are the
men who are denied a satisfying rôle in the western
society which has produced them. For the educated
Africans there is an acute cultural and even personal
loneliness. They are aliens in tribal society. Their
rejection and the discrimination which they experience
confine them to a no man's land in which they live dis-
satisfied and embittered lives. The best of them are
aware of the economic and political concepts which
describe their condition. Many of them are fully aware
of the alternative forms of economic and political action
which communism offers to discontented men. The
relationship which develops between them and the
native population as a whole must be regarded as one
of the most critical questions in South Africa to-day.

To the greater numbers who have only imperfectly
acquired the skills and the ways of the west the frustration may be even more acute since they have less understanding of themselves and their environment. Yet
whatever their status or accomplishment all share in a
growing feeling of resentment. The lowest amongst
them become thieves and criminals. The great majority
of men still stand with an inarticulate African patience
at the gates which bar them. In others, there is already
born a final enmity that scorns compromise, accumulat-

ing within themselves an explosive charge of grievance and passion. Loneliest amongst all of these are the moderate native leaders who still seek the key to compromise and co-operation. As the pathetic shapelessness and inarticulateness of native life yield to greater coherence the new leadership is perforce less moderate and more militant. The area which moderate opinion amongst whites and blacks tried to keep open for debate and co-operation is shrinking into a frontier toxic with hatred. The effort to expel native problems from politics has made them more intensely and dangerously political. Native spokesmen are turned into agitators. Protest against their social and economic plight tends to become illegal and rebellious. Statutory titles such as The Public Safety and Criminal Laws Amendment Acts, the Riotous Assemblies and the Suppression of Communism Acts show the government in the process of manning and fortifying this tragic frontier.

There is a special sum to be drawn between the dignified protests of educated African leaders, the bitter denunciations of half-literate agitators and the endless crimes against life and property which make the nights of the cities so troubled and unsafe. Anger, indignity, and crime add up to a strange but frightening total of protest. Each is an assault upon the prevailing order. Men whose words and purposes are decent are acquiring an unsolicited following of criminals and ruffians. These are beyond their control, yet are an inflammable and explosive ingredient in the rising forces of discontent. A harsh and discriminatory legislation at the top and a grim warfare between the police and crime at the bottom are the closing jaws that seem to be pressing the highest and the lowest in native life into an unwanted but infinitely dangerous alliance.

(YES) It may be wrong or unwise or provocative to speak as yet of chaos or social collapse. Yet if it does take place history tells us something about the manner of its happening. [As Tocqueville pointed out of the French Revolution, some men will act with an extremism and passion that border on madness. Some will invoke religion, or distort it, or deny it. As in Kenya a hatred of western rule will sometimes breed a destructive passion little different from anarchy. We shall see men flash into notoriety as agitators and saboteurs, even as criminals and murderers. Yet all such men and their movements, whether they live briefly, or endure, are the historic agents of the changes at work in the modern world. [If there is enough of wisdom and statesmanship in the western world to deal with these stupendous forces, there must be first of all a recognition that they cannot be simply disciplined by the police, nor will they yield to the restraints of censorship, legal interdiction or any quarantine.] The attentive observer will watch the succession and the trend of those acts where natives individually or concertedly take the initiative in protest or defiance. The catalogue of these acts is already impressive. It is made up of many items small and unobserved, but also of others that reveal an increasing competence to undertake organized action. As long as natives are employed in mines, factories and kitchen, there are no laws that can prevent those multiple acts of resistance and protest which in their accumulation and progression will constitute a major force in the economic and social life of South Africa. In any society where there is a deep resentment it will seek avenues of expression, legal and illegal, visible and invisible, spontaneous and deliberate. [It is yet impossible to tell how long South Africa's malaise will be a slow and chronic debility, or how soon it will become a violent and dangerous inflammation.] *prediction*

(YES) Wise students of the modern world no longer fall into the trap of making <u>communism</u> the cause and explanation of the world's unrest in Africa or Asia. (Yet) at some stage in the analysis of any crisis, whether in Algeria, Indo-China, Kenya or South Africa it is imperative that men remind themselves that the primacy of western thought and practice has been challenged. [The intellectual fervour and the material success of communism have provided the modern world with alternative and competitive methods of thought and action. This has become a world like Europe after Martin Luther. It is a world that is making the reassessments and choices of all great ages of revolution and transition. [In South Africa every man who uses the platform of university, church or press to justify the false economics and dangerous politics of *apartheid*, or to diminish pity and mercy and hope in the conduct of human relations, is widening the door that opens upon the alternative forms of political analysis, social conviction and economic action which communism offers mankind. Such men will be horrified and offended to be seen as the agents of an alternative which they deeply fear and despise. Yet the best allies of revolution are the folly and unwisdom of those who try to sweep back the great tides of historic change. The French Revolution came more inexorably because of the stubbornness and blindness of the eighteenth century aristocracy. "Castes," wrote Jacob Burckhardt, "are absolutely incorrigible even when a large number of their members clearly see the abyss." In South Africa the abyss is plain to see. We are not yet sure how incorrigible is the caste which follows Strydom and Verwoerd.

YES There is intense fear and dislike of communism in South Africa. The laws aimed at its suppression are strenuous. The definition of communism in these laws is so broad that it is possible for any form of agitation or disaffection to be called communistic and so punished. The hostility provoked by militant communism is thoroughly understandable. Yet when the rejection of communism produces also a blindness to the sources and the nature of its appeal, the results in communities like South Africa can be very serious. Few efforts are more rewarding than the effort to see communism through the eyes of a labourer in a Guiana sugar plantation, an Algerian nationalist, or a Malayan peasant living on the edge of starvation. The immense consequences of the Russian Revolution have created new opportunities for men to rise against the heritage of the past. Communism can both be the close ally of revolt or the distant and often indirect cause of disaffection and unrest. According to the experience of all great ages of revolution, men will not always invoke the name or the goals of communism.

Through blindness or selfishness or stupidity western societies can themselves become the most potent allies of the disruption which they most greatly fear. To men who feel themselves despised and rejected, the messianic language of communism holds out the promise of humbling the rich and the mighty, and of renewing the world so as to make place for the downtrodden and the oppressed. They are easily persuaded that the contrast between communism and the west is the contrast between vitality and decay, between humanity and selfishness, between understanding and obtuseness.

It can no longer be taken for granted that the economic and political development of backward peoples can take place only under the influence and within the orbit of the western world. The greatest change which the past generation has seen in communism is its transformation into a massive and compulsive instrument to speed the rise of modern industry, to force inexperienced populations to accept a harsh and laborious existence in the service of industrialization, and to organize powerful political communities. When traditional systems are dissolved by the impact of the west, and when populations are brought to a state of chaos without acquiring a new hopefulness about the future, the west itself paves the way to the communist alternative. A sustained atmosphere of political and social discontent corrodes faith and destroys allegiance.

(YES) Such words as folly and rashness are not too strong to apply to all policies, whether social, economic or political, which refuse to <u>accept Africans as allies and collaborators</u> in the task of building modern economic and political systems.]

(BUT) Upon all men who feel constrained to raise their voices against folly and unwisdom there descends, however, an essential obligation. They must resist the temptation to make unrealistic or merely emotional demands for the solution of Africa's problems. Foreign observers are exposed to the danger of expressing their anxiety in indictments against others or of demanding swift and complete answers to problems that only the succeeding generations can provide. Freedom for Africa instead of injustice, independence instead of oppression seem the correct alternatives to the liberal mind in America or Canada or Great Britain. *(Yet)* all talk of freedom and independence for Africa is misleading unless it is also recognized that the greatest obstacle to these things is <u>African inexperience.</u> It is an unendurable distortion to assume that it is simply the presence of the white man that stands between Africa and political maturity. Through national smugness and a misreading of their own history Americans and Canadians give far too much emphasis to the formal declarations of their own history. A document cannot itself create political maturity. The true meaning of the American Declaration of Independence or the British North America Act is to be found in the political experience, the social stability, the economic advancement and the public

morality that were necessary to sustain and justify them. Political maturity is built on a sufficient foundation of schools and roads, professions and commerce, industry and civil servants, literacy and historical self-awareness, financial integrity, and public honesty. Of all African questions none is more serious than the degree of equation between political aspirations and these fundamentals. Africa needs more of justice and freedom. Yet much of Africa is unready to assume the full responsibility of autonomy. Underdevelopment is the complex result of many deficiencies. Man can be said to be born free only if he is born into a society that can teach him its meaning and train him in its use. That is why it is so deeply important to recognize that the presence and influence of the west are indispensable for the greater freedom and progress which the future may hold.

The backwardness and underdevelopment of Africa can be remedied best by travelling the road pioneered by the west. Modernization in Africa, far more than in India or China, means the acceptance of outside ideas, institutions and skills. A most significant conclusion must therefore be drawn. The European population, above all in South Africa, must not be regarded as alien to Africa, or as nothing more than a foreign ruling class. The whites represent capital investment, science, skills, modern equipment and modern institutions. They are the vehicles and bearers of the very things which Africa needs most. What they have wrought is the indispensable foundation for further progress. The wealth, territorial organization, systems of communications which they have developed are the means by which solutions are to be found for Africa's problems. In the main areas of European settlement such as Kenya, the Rhodesias, and South Africa the withdrawal of the white population is inconceivable. Both the causes and the results of such a contingency would be extreme disaster.

How is Africa to be brought into the modern world and according to which pattern? Is the history of Africa to be hasty and violent, or can it still undergo change by the patient logic of inner growth? These are such urgent questions in Africa and Asia that it is important to see clearly how different these alternatives are. To do this it is illuminating to look briefly once again at the history of change in Great Britain or America and Russia. The real history of Great Britain or America is one of a gradual and prolonged development, as if providence had set aside ample time for the conception of new ideas, the growth of new institutions, and the correction of ancient abuses. In these societies more changes were wrought by an orderly and peaceful accumulation of inner pressures than were violently or abruptly imposed. Those who shared in political debate and who had an influence upon legislation grew in numbers till they comprised the nation. Thus in the long course of generations changes which in their sum were staggering and revolutionary did not lessen political liberties, but actually extended and strengthened them. In Russia, both before and after the Revolution of 1917, change was imposed from above and by means that were coercive. Because it was a backward country, and often a victim of the greater diplomatic and economic power of the western nations, Russia undertook to advance to its coveted economic place by a concentration of the power of the state, acting always in an atmosphere of urgency, and by procedures that were spasmodic and violent. Russia in the description of a perceptive nineteenth-century French traveller, de Custine, "has been deprived . . . of the profound fermentation and the benefit of slow natural development. . . . Adolescence, that laborious age, when the spirit of man assumes entire responsibility for his independence, has been lost to her. Her princes . . . counting time for nothing, made her pass violently from childhood to manhood." In most of Africa there are few problems more urgent than the pace and the manner of needed change. How much time will history give Africa to become divested of its medievalism, its ignorance and its incompetence? How rapidly can it acquire the intellectual and material results of the Renaissance and the Industrial Revolution? Can it pass from childhood to manhood without the cruel forced marches and harsh discipline of tyrannous regimes in a hurry? If there are to be liberal and humane answers to these questions a new body of understandings must come into being. In the very first place a leading responsibility of all government must be a regime of co-operation with the African people in order to secure more health, well-being, hope and goodwill.

It is above all urgent that a real alliance be struck between the whites and emergent African leadership.

That major political and social concessions cannot be
made to a disorganized and primitive native population
cannot justify the arbitrary exclusion in South Africa of
intelligent and educated Africans, Indians and coloured
men from a share in the life of their society. There is
probably no better measure of the unwisdom of South
African policies than the alienation of men in whom
civilization has produced the same mental and spiritual
qualities as mark the white man, to whom words like
hope, freedom and human dignity have the same meaning that they have in England or America. Here all
African territories and governments, certainly south of
the Sahara, are bound together in a common destiny.
The success or failure of self-government in the Gold
Coast, the honesty or the hypocrisy or multi-racial co-
operation in the Central African Federation, the wisdom
or folly of Kenya colonists in settling the Mau Mau
insurrection, the improvement or collapse of racial
relations in South Africa—these are all related fragments
of the total African crisis. At the same time it is clear
that world opinion outside Africa must see Africa in
better perspective and truer proportion. American
senators who clamour for a premature political freedom
when there are no foundations, or Indian nationalists
who denounce all western influence as vicious colonialism, may unwittingly become the sponsors of chaos.
The hour is late, yet even so the greatest danger that
faces Africa is hastiness, either in its own people, or in
those who have taken up the cause of its people. The
South African native population as a whole is in many

Needed

respects the most advanced in Africa. Yet here as elsewhere progress and constructive change depend upon
remaining within the framework of the west.

For the economist the African's road toward progress
and a more modern standard of living is not difficult to
trace. The basic generalizations are clear. Briefly they
are the abandonment of an uneconomical tribal subsistence economy in favour of an exchange and money
economy more able to afford the goods, the skills, the
services and the institutions of a modern society. To the
educated man this statement sounds obvious and sen-
sible. But it means a continuation of social and economic revolution. For the native population it means the
further dissolution of the tribe as a social and economic
organization. It means the far more extensive use of the
land for income and therefore the entry of its products
into the money economy. An emphasis upon the
economic usefulness of land, instead of upon its social
usefulness, must lead to greater individual land tenure,
and a further exodus of the rural tribal population into
the labour market of commerce and industry. In all of
Africa too small a proportion of its resources and of its
manpower is devoted to the profitable production of
goods and services for the market economy of the modern
world. The subsistence economy of the African is totally
unable to bring him sufficient release from ignorance,
disease and privation. Thus more of African agriculture
must become an industry, more Africans must become
wage earners and employees of industry and commerce.
In brief, the African must become modern man. For

the European population, especially in Kenya, the Rhodesias and South Africa, it means the progressive abandonment of arbitrary and pernicious restraints upon the free movement of natives into the activities and opportunities of a modern exchange economy.

What can be simply and directly stated is in reality deeply complex. The prescription of the economists for modern progress is also a verdict that black men must endure the further anguish of disintegration and adjustment, and white men must accept a co-operation which seemed impossible a short generation ago. The reasonable logic of economics asks men to travel a laborious road of hardships and quarrels, and to travel that road at a pace that may often be too urgent for patient reflection and wise action.

When the economist has spoken it is still the historian who has the last word. And the historian's last word is that Africa's most critical need, far transcending all else, is to maintain and greatly extend an atmosphere of confidence between Africa and the west. The security and wellbeing of the white population depend on the wellbeing and security of the native population amongst whom their lot is cast. If the native population can express its political aspirations only in opposition or hostility to the west it will follow that it will regard with fear and suspicion the efforts of the west to develop its resources. Yet without the development of African resources through the use of outside capital and skill, African political aspirations are built on shifting sand.

AFRICA'S MOST CRITICAL NEED

The basic problem in those parts of Africa where black man and white man live together is not one of separation or dissociation, but of co-operation and confidence.

These pages have addressed themselves to the actions of South Africa's white population, and also to the critics of these actions in Great Britain, North America and elsewhere in the western world. It may be appropriate in conclusion to address some words to all, including the African himself. These words come from a very notable document, the *Report of the Royal Commission on East Africa,* "The theme that those who possess an advantage have attained it merely because they belong to a more favoured racial community runs like a pathological obsession throughout the daily life and work of the (native) community. This gives rise in the last resort, to the belief that all would be well if, by a stroke of the pen or the sword, the African could be rid of the presence of the non-African, or could obtain complete political domination over him. Conversely the non-African population seek their security in measures which would prevent such an occurrence and often seek their security in the political domination of the African. Thus tensions . . . are simplified in terms of political power and it is concluded that the problems of . . . Africa are merely political problems which can be settled, and that they can only be settled, by the edicts of political authority, or changes in political and administrative machinery." The African must become modern man. For this to be so, white man and black man in Africa must change and accept change. Those who stand without must facilitate that change in a spirit that is marked by sympathy and generosity towards all.

Printed in Great Britain by The Bowering Press, Plymouth